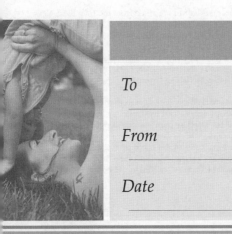

To
_____

From
_____

Date
_____

199 Favorite Bible Verses for Busy Moms

© 2010 Christian Art Gifts, RSA
        Christian Art Gifts Inc., IL, USA

Designed by Christian Art Gifts

Images used under license from Shutterstock.com

Scripture quotations marked NIV are taken from the *Holy Bible*,
New International Version® NIV®. Copyright © 1973, 1978, 1984
by International Bible Society. Used by permission of Zondervan
Publishing House. All rights reserved.

Scripture quotations marked NLT are taken from the *Holy Bible*, New
Living Translation®, second edition. Copyright © 1996, 2004 by Tyndale
House Publishers, Inc., Carol Stream, Illinois 60188. All rights reserved.

Scripture quotations marked THE MESSAGE are taken from *The Message*.
Copyright © by Eugene H. Peterson, 1993, 1994, 1995. Used by
permission of NavPress Publishing Group.

Scripture quotations marked ESV are taken from the *Holy Bible*, English
Standard Version. Copyright © 2001 by Crossway Bibles, a division of
Good News Publishers. Used by permission. All rights reserved.

Scripture quotations marked NCV are taken from the *Holy Bible*,
New Century Version®. Copyright © 1987, 1988, 1991, 2005 by Word
Publishing, a division of Thomas Nelson, Inc. Used by permission.

Printed in China

ISBN 978-1-77036-439-4

10 11 12 13 14 15 16 17 18 19 – 12 11 10 9 8 7 6 5 4 3

199 *favorite*
Bible verses for
busy moms

christian
art gifts®

Contents

1. Wake Up Call
   Scripture to Help You Start the Day Right

   Encouragement.................. 9
   Gratitude 13
   Joy 17

2. Is this Really My Life?
   *Scripture to Help You Get through
   the Day*

   Comfort............................. 23
   Endurance........................ 27
   God's Love 31
   Hope 35
   Strength............................ 39

3. Mom-on-the-Go
   Loving Being a Mom

   Fulfillment 45
   The Joys of Motherhood ... 49

4. The Fabric of a Mother
   What Makes You a Mother?

   Friends 55
   Husband 59
   Kids 63

5. Motherly Duties
   Be the Best Mom That You Can Be

   Be a Loving Example......... 69
   Have Patience 73
   Raise Godly Kids................. 77
   Serve Your Family 81
   Try Conflict Resolution 83

6. Time-Outs
   Godly Help to Cope with Crises

   Prayer 89
   Rest 93
   Time with God 95

7. Family Life
   Scripture on Matters of the Heart

   Guidance 101
   Health............................... 103
   Marriage 107
   Money Matters................. 111
   Wisdom 115

8. We Are Family
   Scripture for Making You a Strong Family Unit

   A Godly Home 121
   Unity.................................. 125

Wake Up Call

*Scripture to Help You
Start the Day Right*

*I still find each day too short for

all the thoughts I want to think,

all the walks I want to take,

all the books I want to read and

all the friends I want to see.*

John Burroughs

When you feel like giving up,
remember why you held on
for so long in the first place.

Anonymous

Encouragement

1

The LORD your God is in your midst, a mighty One who will save; He will rejoice over you with gladness; He will quiet you by His love; He will exult over you with loud singing.

Zephaniah 3:17 ESV

2

The faithful love of the LORD never ends! His mercies never cease. Great is His faithfulness; His mercies begin afresh each morning.

Lamentations 3:22-23 NLT

3

"Not by might nor by power, but by My Spirit," says the LORD Almighty.

Zechariah 4:6 NIV

Encouragement

4

Delight yourself in the LORD and He will give you the desires of your heart.

Psalm 37:4 NIV

5

May our Lord Jesus Christ Himself, who loved us and by His grace gave us eternal encouragement and good hope, encourage your hearts and strengthen you in every good deed and word.

2 Thessalonians 2:16-17 NIV

6

Blessings crown the head of the righteous.

Proverbs 10:6 NIV

7

The Scriptures give us hope and encouragement as we wait patiently for God's promises to be fulfilled.

Romans 15:4 NLT

Instead of giving myself reasons why I can't; I give myself reasons why I can.

Anonymous

At times our own light goes out and is rekindled by a spark from another person. Each of us has cause to think with deep gratitude of those who have lighted the flame within us.

Albert Schweitzer

Gratitude

8

Since everything God created is good, we should not reject any of it, but receive it with thanks.

1 Timothy 4:4 NLT

9

Be joyful always, pray continually, give thanks in all circumstances; for this is God's will for you in Christ Jesus.

1 Thessalonians 5:16-18 NIV

10

I will give thanks to the LORD with my whole heart; I will recount all of Your wonderful deeds.

Psalm 9:1 ESV

Gratitude

11

Let your roots grow down into Him, and let your lives be built on Him. Then your faith will grow strong in the truth you were taught, and you will overflow with thankfulness.

Colossians 2:7 NLT

12

The LORD is good and His love endures forever; His faithfulness continues through all generations.

Psalm 100:5 NIV

13

Light is shed upon the righteous and joy on the upright in heart.

Psalm 97:11 NIV

14

No eye has seen, no ear has heard, and no mind has imagined what God has prepared for those who love Him.

1 Corinthians 2:9 NLT

15

A cheerful heart fills the day with song.

Proverbs 15:15 THE MESSAGE

May your walls know joy;
may every room hold
laughter and every window
open to great possibility.

Maryanne Radmacher-Hershey

Joy

16

This is the day the LORD has made; let us rejoice and be glad in it.

Psalm 118:24 NIV

17

In Him our hearts rejoice, for we trust in His holy name.

Psalm 33:21 NLT

18

I am overwhelmed with joy in the LORD my God!

Isaiah 61:10 NLT

19

The joy of the LORD is your strength.

Nehemiah 8:10 ESV

Joy

20

Let all who take refuge in You be glad;
let them ever sing for joy. Spread Your
protection over them, that those who
love Your name may rejoice in You.

Psalm 5:11 NIV

21

Satisfy us in the morning with Your
steadfast love, that we may rejoice
and be glad all our days.

Psalm 90:14 ESV

22

I know the LORD is always with me.
No wonder my heart is glad, and I
rejoice.

Psalm 16:8-9 NLT

23

Rejoice in the Lord always.

Philippians 4:4 NIV

24

The Holy Spirit produces this kind of fruit in our lives: joy.

Galatians 5:22 NLT

Joy is the echo of God's life within us.

Joseph Marmion

The greatest part
of our happiness
depends on our dispositions,
not our circumstances.

Martha Washington

Is this Really My Life?

Scripture to Help You
Get through the Day

The sun can break

through the darkest cloud;

love can brighten

the gloomiest day.

William Arthur Ward

Comfort

25

May Your unfailing love be my comfort, according to Your promise to Your servant.

Psalm 119:76 NIV

26

The more we suffer for Christ, the more God will shower us with His comfort through Christ.

2 Corinthians 1:5 NLT

27

If your heart is broken, you'll find GOD right there; if you're kicked in the gut, He'll help you catch your breath.

Psalm 34:18 THE MESSAGE

Comfort

28

"As a mother comforts her child, so will I comfort you."

Isaiah 66:13 NIV

29

Those who plant in tears will harvest with shouts of joy.

Psalm 126:5 NLT

30

God heals the brokenhearted and binds up their wounds.

Psalm 147:3 NIV

31

Weeping may last through the night, but joy comes with the morning.

Psalm 30:5 NLT

Comfort

32

"I'll be with you, day after day after
day, right up to the end of the age."

Matthew 28:20 THE MESSAGE

In Christ the heart of the Father
is revealed, and higher comfort
there cannot be than to rest
in the Father's heart.

Andrew Murray

Endurance is not just
the ability to bear a hard thing,
but to turn it into glory.

William Barclay

Endurance

33

You need to persevere so that when you have done the will of God, you will receive what He has promised.

Hebrews 10:36 NIV

34

Let us not grow weary of doing good, for in due season we will reap, if we do not give up.

Galatians 6:9 ESV

35

God blesses those who patiently endure testing and temptation. Afterward they will receive the crown of life that God has promised to those who love Him.

James 1:12 NLT

Endurance

36

There has never been the slightest doubt in my mind that the God who started this great work in you would keep at it and bring it to a flourishing finish.

Philippians 1:6 THE MESSAGE

37

"I will refresh the weary and satisfy the faint."

Jeremiah 31:25 NIV

38

Be truly glad. There is wonderful joy ahead, even though you have to endure many trials for a little while.

1 Peter 1:6 NLT

Endurance

39

People with their minds set on You, You keep completely whole, steady on their feet, because they keep at it and don't quit. Depend on God and keep at it because in the Lord God you have a sure thing.

Isaiah 26:3-4 THE MESSAGE

40

We rejoice in our sufferings, because we know that suffering produces perseverance; perseverance, character; and character, hope. And hope does not disappoint us.

Romans 5:3-5 NIV

*Though our feelings
come and go, God's love
for us does not.*

C. S. Lewis

God's Love

41

Nothing in all creation will ever be able to separate us from the love of God.

Romans 8:39 NLT

42

God's love is meteoric, His loyalty astronomic, His purpose titanic, His verdicts oceanic. Yet in His largeness nothing gets lost; not a man, not a mouse, slips through the cracks.

Psalm 36:5-6 THE MESSAGE

43

"I lavish unfailing love for a thousand generations on those who love Me and obey My commands."

Deuteronomy 5:10 NLT

44

"When you come looking for Me, you'll find Me. Yes, when you get serious about finding Me and want it more than anything else, I'll make sure you won't be disappointed. I'll turn things around for you."

Jeremiah 29:13-14 THE MESSAGE

45

May you experience the love of Christ, though it is too great to understand fully. Then you will be made complete with all the fullness of life and power that comes from God.

Ephesians 3:19 NLT

God's Love

46

How blessed is God! Long before He laid down earth's foundations, He had us in mind, had settled on us as the focus of His love, to be made whole and holy by His love.

Ephesians 1:3-5 THE MESSAGE

47

The LORD says, "I will rescue those who love Me. I will protect those who trust in My name."

Psalm 91:14 NLT

48

You are a chosen people. You are royal priests, a holy nation, God's very own possession. He called you out of the darkness into His wonderful light.

1 Peter 2:9 NLT

When the world says,

"Give up,"

Hope whispers,

"Try it one more time."

Anonymous

Hope

49

The LORD is good to those whose hope is in Him.

Lamentations 3:25 NIV

50

May the God of hope fill you up with joy, fill you up with peace, so that your believing lives, filled with the life-giving energy of the Holy Spirit, will brim over with hope!

Romans 15:13 THE MESSAGE

51

We rejoice in the hope of the glory of God. And hope does not disappoint us, because God has poured out His love into our hearts by the Holy Spirit, whom He has given us.

Romans 5:2, 5 NIV

52

There is surely a future hope for you,
and your hope will not be cut off.

Proverbs 23:18 NIV

53

Hope deferred makes the heart sick,
but a desire fulfilled is a tree of life.

Proverbs 13:12 ESV

54

I wait for the Lord, my soul waits, and
in His word I put my hope.

Psalm 130:5 NIV

55

No one whose hope is in God will
ever be put to shame.

Psalm 25:3 NIV

56

Let us hold tightly without wavering to the hope we affirm, for God can be trusted to keep His promise.

Hebrews 10:23 NLT

If you lose hope, somehow you lose the vitality that keeps life moving, you lose that courage to be, that quality that helps you go on in spite of it all.

Martin Luther King, Jr.

*Let me tell you the secret
that has led me to my goal.
My strength lies solely
in my tenacity.*

Louis Pasteur

Strength

57

I can do everything through Him who gives me strength.

Philippians 4:13 NIV

58

The LORD is my strength and shield from every danger. I trust Him with all my heart.

Psalm 28:7 NLT

59

Those who hope in the LORD will renew their strength. They will soar on wings like eagles; they will run and not grow weary, they will walk and not be faint.

Isaiah 40:31 NIV

60

The LORD gives His people strength.
The LORD blesses them with peace.

Psalm 29:11 NLT

61

"Do not fear, for I am with you; do
not be dismayed, for I am your God.
I will strengthen you and help you;
I will uphold you with My righteous
right hand."

Isaiah 41:10 NIV

62

God is our refuge and strength, a
very present help in trouble.

Psalm 46:1 ESV

63

"In repentance and rest is your salvation, in quietness and trust is your strength."

Isaiah 30:15 NIV

64

She sets about her work vigorously; her arms are strong for her tasks.

Proverbs 31:17 NIV

Of all the rights
of women, the greatest is
to be a mother.

Anonymous

Mom-on-the-Go

Loving Being a Mom

Look at a day when you are

supremely satisfied at the end.

It's not a day when you lounge

around doing nothing;

it's when you've

had everything to do,

and you've done it.

Margaret Thatcher

Fulfillment

65

"I know the plans I have for you," declares the LORD, "plans to prosper you and not to harm you, plans to give you hope and a future."

Jeremiah 29:11 NIV

66

The LORD called me before my birth; from within the womb He called me by name.

Isaiah 49:1 NLT

67

The LORD will fulfill His purpose for me; Your steadfast love, O LORD, endures forever. Do not forsake the work of Your hands.

Psalm 138:8 ESV

68

"I came to give life – life in all its fullness."

John 10:10 NCV

69

I have learned in whatever situation I am to be content. I can do all things through Him who strengthens me.

Philippians 4:11, 13 ESV

70

I will be glad and rejoice in Your unfailing love, for You have seen my troubles, and You care about the anguish of my soul.

Psalm 31:7 NLT

71

The LORD is my shepherd, I shall not be in want.

Psalm 23:1 NIV

72

An appetite for good brings much satisfaction.

Proverbs 13:25 THE MESSAGE

God could not be everywhere and therefore He made mothers.

Jewish Proverb

The Joys of Motherhood

73

Her children arise and call her blessed; her husband also, and he praises her.

Proverbs 31:28 NIV

74

Nothing gives me greater joy than to hear that my children are following the way of truth.

3 John 4 NCV

75

"Don't get worked up about what may or may not happen tomorrow. God will help you deal with whatever hard things come up when the time comes."

Matthew 6:34 THE MESSAGE

76

Children are a gift from the LORD; babies are a reward.

Psalm 127:3 NCV

77

Grandchildren are the crowning glory of the aged; parents are the pride of their children.

Proverbs 17:6 NLT

78

Be content with who you are, and don't put on airs. God's strong hand is on you; He'll promote you at the right time. Live carefree before God; He is most careful with you.

1 Peter 5:6 THE MESSAGE

Children are the anchors

that hold a mother to life.

Sophocles

*Maternal love
is a miraculous substance
that God multiplies
as He divides it.*

Victor Hugo

The Fabric of a Mother

What Makes You a Mother?

A faithful friend

is an image of God.

French Proverb

Friends

79

"Where two or three are gathered in My name, there am I among them."

Matthew 18:20 ESV

80

Join the company of good men and women, keep your feet on the tried-and-true paths.

Proverbs 2:20 THE MESSAGE

81

"I give you a new command: Love each other. You must love each other as I have loved you. All people will know that you are My followers if you love each other."

John 13:34-35 NCV

Friends

82

The one who blesses others is abundantly blessed; those who help others are helped.

Proverbs 11:25 THE MESSAGE

83

You use steel to sharpen steel, and one friend sharpens another.

Proverbs 27:17 THE MESSAGE

84

Friends come and friends go, but a true friend sticks by you like family.

Proverbs 18:24 THE MESSAGE

85

The heartfelt counsel of a friend is as sweet as perfume and incense.

Proverbs 27:9 NLT

A true friend is one who knows all about you and likes you anyway.

Christi Mary Warner

A woman who treasures,
respects and honors
her husband is a Queen
in his eyes.

Anonymous

Husband

86

Find a good spouse, you find a good life – and even more: the favor of GOD!

Proverbs 18:22 THE MESSAGE

87

A wife of noble character is her husband's crown, but a disgraceful wife is like decay in his bones.

Proverbs 12:4 NIV

88

A wife is bound to her husband as long as he lives.

1 Corinthians 7:39 NLT

89

Wives, submit to your own husbands, as to the Lord. For the husband is the head of the wife.

Ephesians 5:22 ESV

90

A wife must respect her husband.

Ephesians 5:33 NCV

91

Love each other with genuine affection, and take delight in honoring each other.

Romans 12:10 NLT

A perfect wife is one

who doesn't expect

a perfect husband.

Anonymous

The soul is healed

by being with children.

Fyodor Dostoevsky

Kids

92

"Let the little children come to Me, and do not hinder them, for the kingdom of heaven belongs to such as these."

Matthew 19:14 NIV

93

"Whoever embraces one of these children as I do embraces Me, and far more than Me – God who sent Me."

Mark 9:36-37 THE MESSAGE

94

I prayed for this child, and the Lord has granted me what I asked of Him. So now I give him to the Lord. For his whole life he will be given over to the Lord.

1 Samuel 1:27-28 NIV

95

"Can a woman forget the baby she nurses? Can she feel no kindness for the child to which she gave birth?"

Isaiah 49:15 NCV

96

The Lord says, "As surely as I live, your children will be like jewels that a bride wears proudly."

Isaiah 49:18 NCV

While we try to teach our children all about life, our children teach us what life is all about.

Angela Schwindt

One good mother is worth

a hundred schoolmasters.

George Herbert

Motherly Duties

Be the Best Mom
That You Can Be

Children need models more than they need critics.

Joseph Joubert

Be a Loving Example

97

The ways of right-living people glow with light; the longer they live, the brighter they shine.

Proverbs 4:18 THE MESSAGE

98

Don't lose sight of common sense and discernment. Hang on to them, for they will refresh your soul.

Proverbs 3:21-22 NLT

99

In every way be an example of doing good deeds. When you teach, do it with honesty and seriousness.

Titus 2:7 NCV

Be a Loving Example

100

The Lord approves of those who are good.

Proverbs 12:2 NLT

101

Wise living gets rewarded with honor; stupid living gets the booby prize.

Proverbs 3:35 THE MESSAGE

102

Hate what is wrong. Hold tightly to what is good.

Romans 12:9 NLT

103

Do everything in love.

1 Corinthians 16:14 NIV

Be a Loving Example

104

She speaks with wisdom, and faithful instruction is on her tongue.

Proverbs 31:26 NIV

105

Trouble chases sinners, while blessings reward the righteous.

Proverbs 13:21 NLT

Be as patient with others

as God has been with you.

Anonymous

Have Patience

106

I waited patiently for the LORD; He inclined to me and heard my cry.

Psalm 40:1 ESV

107

If you suffer for doing good and endure it patiently, God is pleased with you.

1 Peter 2:20 NLT

108

We continue to shout our praise even when we're hemmed in with troubles, because we know how troubles can develop passionate patience in us, and how that patience in turn forges the tempered steel of virtue, keeping us alert for whatever God will do next.

Romans 5:3-4 THE MESSAGE

109

Be still before the LORD and wait patiently for Him. Those who wait for the LORD shall inherit the land.

Psalm 37:7, 9 ESV

110

God proves to be good to the one who diligently seeks. It's a good thing to quietly hope, quietly hope for help from God.

Lamentations 3:25-26 THE MESSAGE

111

Be patient in tribulation, be constant in prayer.

Romans 12:12 ESV

Have Patience

112

May the Lord direct your hearts to the love of God and to the steadfastness of Christ.

2 Thessalonians 3:5 ESV

113

The longer we wait, the more joyful our expectancy.

Romans 8:25 THE MESSAGE

There are two

lasting bequests we

can give our children.

One is roots.

The other is wings.

Hodding Carter, Jr.

Raise Godly Kids

114

Train a child in the way he should go, and when he is old he will not turn from it.

Proverbs 22:6 NIV

115

My child, listen to me and do as I say, and you will have a long, good life. I will teach you wisdom's ways and lead you in straight paths.

Proverbs 4:10-11 NLT

116

My child, pay attention to my words; listen closely to what I say. Don't ever forget my words; keep them always in mind. They are the key to life for those who find them; they bring health to the whole body.

Proverbs 4:20-22 NCV

117

Do not exasperate your children; instead, bring them up in the training and instruction of the Lord.

Ephesians 6:4 NIV

118

We can see who God's children are: Those who do not do what is right are not God's children, and those who do not love their brothers and sisters are not God's children.

1 John 3:10 NCV

119

All Scripture is inspired by God and is useful to teach us what is true. It corrects us when we are wrong and teaches us to do what is right.

2 Timothy 3:16 NLT

120

If you do not punish your children, you don't love them, but if you love your children, you will correct them.

Proverbs 13:24 NCV

Other things may change us,

but we start and

end with family.

Anthony Brandt

Serve Your Family

121

"If you try to hang on to your life, you will lose it. But if you give up your life for My sake, you will save it."

Matthew 16:25 NLT

122

"Now that I, your Lord and Teacher, have washed your feet, you also should wash one another's feet."

John 13:14 NIV

123

God loves a cheerful giver. And God is able to provide you with every blessing in abundance, so that having all sufficiency in all things at all times, you may abound in every good work.

2 Corinthians 9:7-8 ESV

124

"Whoever wants to be great among you must serve the rest like a servant. In the same way, the Son of Man did not come to be served. He came to serve others and to give His life as a ransom for many people."

Matthew 20:26, 28 NCV

125

"Give, and you will receive. Your gift will return to you in full. The amount you give will determine the amount you get back."

Luke 6:38 NLT

126

Love always looks for the best, never looks back, but keeps going to the end.

1 Corinthians 13:7 THE MESSAGE

Try Conflict Resolution

127

"Love your neighbor as yourself."

Matthew 19:19 ESV

128

Do not let the sun go down while you are still angry.

Ephesians 4:26 NIV

129

Control your temper, for anger labels you a fool.

Ecclesiastes 7:9 NLT

130

A gentle answer will calm a person's anger, but an unkind answer will cause more anger.

Proverbs 15:1 NCV

131

Love one another deeply, from the heart.

1 Peter 1:22 NIV

132

If anyone slaps you on one cheek, offer him the other cheek, too.

Luke 6:29 NCV

133

Do everything in love.

1 Corinthians 16:14 NIV

134

Cast all your anxiety on Him because He cares for you.

1 Peter 5:7 NIV

Peace reigns

where our Lord reigns.

Julian of Norwich

The love of God is broader

than the measures

of man's mind; and the heart

of the Eternal is most

wonderfully kind.

F. W. Faber

Time-Outs

Godly Help
   to Cope with Crises

To pray is to mount on eagle's wings above the clouds and get into the clear heaven where God dwells.

Charles H. Spurgeon

Prayer

135

The eyes of the Lord are on the right-eous, and His ears are open to their prayer.

1 Peter 3:12 ESV

136

Pray for each other. The earnest prayer of a righteous person has great power and produces wonder-ful results.

James 5:16 NLT

137

Give attention to Your servant's prayer, O LORD my God. Hear the cry and the prayer that Your servant is praying in Your presence.

2 Chronicles 6:19 NIV

138

"Whatever you ask for in prayer, believe that you have received it, and it will be yours."

Mark 11:24 NIV

139

God's there, listening for all who pray, for all who pray and mean it.

Psalm 145:18 THE MESSAGE

140

"Call upon Me in the day of trouble; I will deliver you, and you will honor Me."

Psalm 50:15 NIV

Prayer

141

God's Spirit is right alongside helping us along. If we don't know how or what to pray, it doesn't matter. He does our praying in and for us, making prayer out of our wordless sighs, our aching groans. He knows us far better than we know ourselves and keeps us present before God.

Romans 8:26-27 THE MESSAGE

142

In the morning, O LORD, You hear my voice; in the morning I lay my requests before You and wait in expectation.

Psalm 5:3 NIV

You have made us for

Yourself, and our heart

cannot be stilled until

it finds rest in You.

St. Augustine

Rest

143

The LORD is my shepherd, I shall not be in want. He makes me lie down in green pastures, He leads me beside quiet waters, He restores my soul.

Psalm 23:1-3 NIV

144

"Come to Me, all who labor and are heavy laden, and I will give you rest. You will find rest for your souls."

Matthew 11:28-29 ESV

145

"My people will live in peaceful places and in safe homes and in calm places of rest."

Isaiah 32:18 NCV

Rest

146

"On the seventh day God rested from all His work."

Hebrews 4:4 NIV

147

Don't you know God enjoys giving rest to those He loves?

Psalm 127:2 THE MESSAGE

148

I can lie down and go to sleep, and I will wake up again, because the LORD gives me strength.

Psalm 3:5 NCV

Time with God

149

I love Your clear-cut revelation. You're my place of quiet retreat; I wait for Your Word to renew me.

Psalm 119:113-114 THE MESSAGE

150

"Live in Me. Make your home in Me. If you make yourselves at home with Me and My words are at home in you, you can be sure that whatever you ask will be listened to and acted upon."

John 15:4, 7 THE MESSAGE

151

"It takes more than bread to stay alive. It takes a steady stream of words from God's mouth."

Matthew 4:4 THE MESSAGE

Time with God

152

The LORD is with you while you are with Him. If you seek Him, He will be found by you.

2 Chronicles 15:2 ESV

153

I pray to God – my life a prayer – and wait for what He'll say and do. My life's on the line before God, my Lord, waiting and watching till morning.

Psalm 130:5-6 THE MESSAGE

154

Let us draw near to God, with a sincere heart in full assurance of faith.

Hebrews 10:22 NIV

155

As a deer pants for flowing streams, so pants my soul for You, O God. My soul thirsts for God, for the living God. When shall I come and appear before God?

Psalm 42:1-2 ESV

156

Your words are my joy and my heart's delight.

Jeremiah 15:16 NLT

157

The Word of the LORD is right and true; He is faithful in all He does.

Psalm 33:4 NIV

I need nothing but God,

and to lose myself

in the heart of Jesus.

Margaret Mary Alacoque

Family Life

Scripture on Matters
of the Heart

Seek God first in all you do –

then His light will shine

on the road you should take.

Anonymous

Guidance

158

The LORD says, "I will guide you along the best pathway for your life. I will advise you and watch over you."

Psalm 32:8 NLT

159

"Call to Me and I will answer you, and will tell you great and hidden things that you have not known."

Jeremiah 33:3 ESV

160

We do not have a High Priest who is unable to sympathize with our weaknesses. Let us then with confidence draw near to the throne of grace, that we may receive mercy and find grace to help in time of need.

Hebrews 4:15-16 ESV

Guidance

161

The LORD directs the steps of the godly. He delights in every detail of their lives.

Psalm 37:23 NLT

162

Show me the right path, O LORD; point out the road for me to follow.

Psalm 25:4 NLT

163

The LORD will guide you always.

Isaiah 58:11 NIV

164

"I know His commands lead to eternal life; so I say whatever the Father tells Me to say."

John 12:50 NLT

Health

165

"I will give you back your health and heal your wounds," says the LORD.

Jeremiah 30:17 NLT

166

He was wounded for the wrong we did; He was crushed for the evil we did. The punishment, which made us well, was given to Him, and we are healed because of His wounds.

Isaiah 53:5 NCV

167

"The sun of righteousness will dawn on those who honor My name, healing radiating from its wings. You will be bursting with energy."

Malachi 4:3 THE MESSAGE

168

"I am the LORD who heals you."

Exodus 15:26 NCV

169

Those who look to Him for help will be radiant with joy; no shadow of shame will darken their faces.

Psalm 34:5 NLT

When wealth is lost, nothing is lost;
when health is lost, something is lost;
when character is lost, all is lost.

Billy Graham

*If you have health,
you will probably be happy,
and if you have health
and happiness, you have all
the wealth you need,
even if it is not all you want.*

Elbert Hubbard

Be the mate God designed you to be.

Anthony T. Evans

Marriage

170

Most important of all, continue to show deep love for each other, for love covers a multitude of sins.

1 Peter 4:8 NLT

171

Be sure to stop being angry before the end of the day.

Ephesians 4:26 NCV

172

May the patience and encouragement that come from God allow you to live in harmony with each other the way Christ Jesus wants. Then you will be joined together, and you will give glory to God.

Romans 15:5-6 NCV

173

Love is patient and kind. It is not irritable, and it keeps no record of being wronged. Love never gives up, never loses faith, is always hopeful, and endures through every circumstance.

1 Corinthians 13:4-5, 7 NLT

174

Give honor to marriage, and remain faithful to one another in marriage.

Hebrews 13:4 NLT

175

May the Lord make you increase and abound in love for one another.

1 Thessalonians 3:12 ESV

176

The Christian wife brings holiness to her marriage, and the Christian husband brings holiness to his marriage.

1 Corinthians 7:14 NLT

Trust God to provide all your needs – He has a never-ending supply of resources at His disposal, and He loves to share.

Anonymous

Money Matters

177

God will use His wonderful riches in Christ Jesus to give you everything you need.

Philippians 4:19 NCV

178

"If God cares so wonderfully for wildflowers that are here today and thrown into the fire tomorrow, He will certainly care for you. Seek the Kingdom of God above all else, and live righteously, and He will give you everything you need."

Matthew 6:30, 33 NLT

179

Submit to God and be at peace with Him; in this way prosperity will come to you.

Job 22:21 NIV

180

"Bring the whole tithe into the storehouse, that there may be food in My house. Test Me in this," says the LORD Almighty, "and see if I will not throw open the floodgates of heaven and pour out so much blessing that you will not have room enough for it."

Malachi 3:10 NIV

181

The LORD is my chosen portion and my cup; You hold my lot. The lines have fallen for me in pleasant places; I have a beautiful inheritance.

Psalm 16:5-6 ESV

182

Honor God with everything you own; give Him the first and the best. Your barns will burst, your wine vats will brim over.

Proverbs 3:9-10 THE MESSAGE

If you want to feel rich,
just count all the things you have
that money can't buy.

Anonymous

True wisdom is

gazing at God.

Isaac the Syrian

Wisdom

183

If you need wisdom, ask our gener-
ous God, and He will give it to you.
He will not rebuke you for asking.

James 1:5 NLT

184

Wisdom will multiply your days and
add years to your life.

Proverbs 9:11 NLT

185

If you call out for insight and raise
your voice for understanding, if you
seek it like silver and search for it as for
hidden treasures, then you will find
the knowledge of God.

Proverbs 2:3-5 ESV

186

Wisdom is sweet to your soul. If you find it, you will have a bright future, and your hopes will not be cut short.

Proverbs 24:14 NLT

187

Real wisdom, God's wisdom, begins with a holy life and is characterized by getting along with others. It is gentle and reasonable, overflowing with mercy and blessings.

James 3:17 THE MESSAGE

188

"I will give you a wise and discerning heart, so that there will never have been anyone like you."

1 Kings 3:12 NIV

We are made wise not by

the recollection of our past,

but by the responsibility

for our future.

George Bernard Shaw

*The family was ordained
by God before He established
any other institution,
even before He established
the church.*

Billy Graham

We Are Family

Scripture for Making You
a Strong Family Unit

The goal of every married couple, indeed, every Christian home, should be to make Christ the Head, the Counselor and the Guide.

Paul Sadler

A Godly Home

189

As for me and my household, we will serve the LORD.

Joshua 24:15 NIV

190

Jesus replied, "All who love Me will do what I say. My Father will love them, and We will come and make Our home with each of them."

John 14:23 NLT

191

Don't for a minute let this Book of The Revelation be out of mind. Ponder and meditate on it day and night, making sure you practice everything written in it.

Joshua 1:8 THE MESSAGE

A Godly Home

192

"I will be a father to you, and you shall be sons and daughters to Me," says the Lord Almighty.

2 Corinthians 6:18 ESV

193

Bow in prayer before the Father from whom every family in heaven and on earth gets its true name.

Ephesians 3:14-15 NCV

194

I look up to the mountains – does my help come from there? My help comes from the LORD, who made heaven and earth!

Psalm 121:1-2 NLT

All the wealth in the world

cannot be compared with the

happiness of living together

happily united.

Margaret of Youville

If we focus on differences

our focus is on each other.

If we focus with unity,

our focus is on God.

Anonymous

Unity

195

Be of one mind, live in peace. And the God of love and peace will be with you.

2 Corinthians 13:11 NIV

196

There are different kinds of service, but the same Lord.

1 Corinthians 12:5 NIV

197

"I in them and You in Me. May they be brought to complete unity to let the world know that You sent Me and have loved them even as You have loved Me."

John 17:23 NIV

Unity

198

It is good and pleasant when God's people live together in peace! There the LORD gives His blessing of life forever.

Psalm 133:1, 3 NCV

199

You are joined together with peace through the Spirit, so make every effort to continue together in this way.

Ephesians 4:3 NCV

Everyone has inside them

a piece of good news.

The good news is you don't

know how great you can be!

How much you can love!

What you can accomplish!

And what your potential is!

Anne Frank